I0163100

# OXFORD PAMPHLETS
# 1914–1915

# ALSACE-LORRAINE

BY

F. Y. ECCLES

*Price Twopence net*

OXFORD UNIVERSITY PRESS
HUMPHREY MILFORD
LONDON  EDINBURGH  GLASGOW
NEW YORK  TORONTO  MELBOURNE  BOMBAY

# ALSACE-LORRAINE

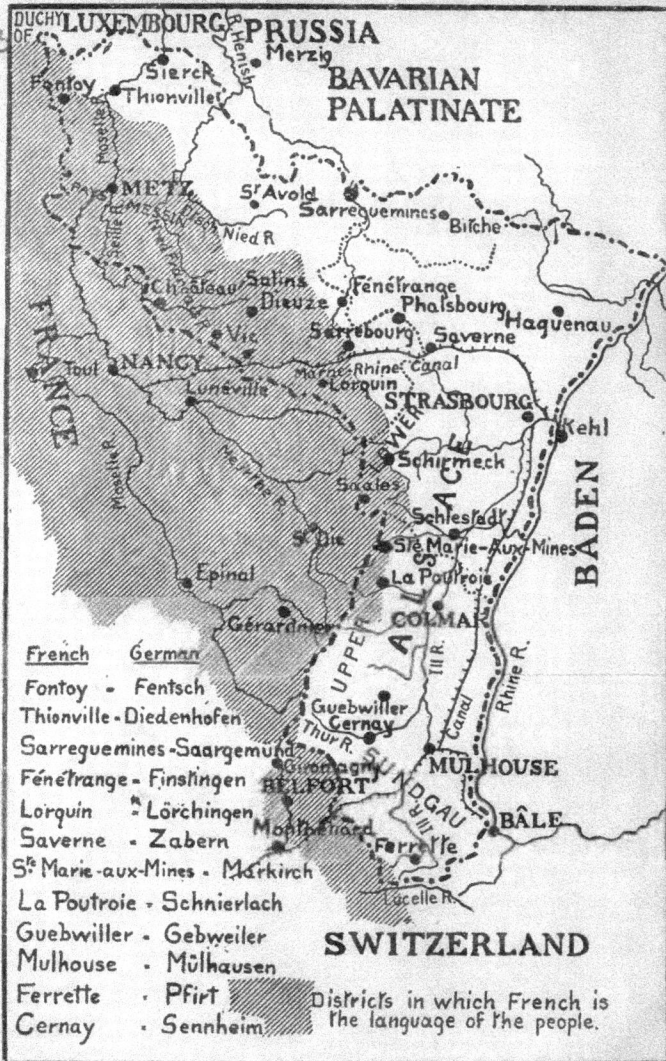

DUCHY OF LUXEMBOURG — PRUSSIA

BAVARIAN PALATINATE

Fontoy · Sierck · Merzig · Thionville

FRANCE

METZ · St Avold · Sarreguemines · Bitche · Nied R.

Château Salins · Dieuze · Fénétrange · Phalsbourg · Haguenau · Vic · Sarrebourg · Saverne

Toul · NANCY · Lunéville · Lorquin · Marne-Rhine Canal · STRASBOURG · Kehl

Moselle R. · Meurthe R. · Saales · Schirmeck · La Bruche

St Dié · Schlestadt · Ste Marie-aux-Mines · La Poutroie

Épinal · Gérardmer · COLMAR · Ill R.

UPPER ALSACE · Rhine R. · Canal

French · German

Fontoy · Fentsch
Thionville · Diedenhofen
Sarreguemines · Saargemünd
Fénétrange · Finstingen
Lorquin · Lörchingen
Saverne · Zabern
Ste Marie-aux-Mines · Markirch
La Poutroie · Schnierlach
Guebwiller · Gebweiler
Mulhouse · Mülhausen
Ferrette · Pfirt
Cernay · Sennheim

Guebwiller · Cernay · Thur R. · Giromagny · BELFORT · MULHOUSE · Montbéliard · Ferrette · BÂLE · SUNDGAU · Largelle R.

BADEN

SWITZERLAND

Districts in which French is the language of the people.

# ALSACE-LORRAINE

FRANCE is not at war about Alsace-Lorraine, but nobody doubts that if the Germans are beaten she will get back the provinces torn from her forty-four years ago. Her sacrifices, her credit, her security require their restitution, and since an unprovoked attack upon her has revived the memory of her bitterest humiliation, her people will be content with nothing less. But French pride and French power are not alone concerned. There is a sense of justice to be satisfied, and the desire for a lasting settlement. Perhaps some Englishmen are a little doubtful (though their sympathies are heartily with our Ally) whether a better could not be devised in the interest both of the inhabitants and of European tranquillity. They have been told that the problem is delicate and complex. It is clearly less simple than it was before the German experiment, which has failed, but has inevitably introduced new factors. Is there no case for compromise, for an equitable partition, or for the establishment of a neutral ' buffer ' state ?

Before attempting to answer this question, let us go back to the Treaty of Frankfort (May 10, 1871), by which Alsace-Lorraine, the Reichsland, came into being. The Germans, when they exacted the surrender of French territory [1] as part of the price of peace, did nothing for which history does not furnish precedents in plenty ;

[1] It comprised the department of the Lower Rhine, almost all that of the Upper Rhine, more than half the department of the Moselle, a third of the Meurthe and a corner of the Vosges. All the Alsace of history, except Belfort, is included in this territory, and about the third part of the Duchy of Lorraine, with Metz and the Pays Messin

they only denied—in contradiction to the spirit of the
time—the right of human groups, conscious of a collec-
tive personality, to dispose of themselves and to choose
their allegiance.  This right, which could have no mean-
ing while national sentiment was weak and vacillating
and the desires of subjects inarticulate, had gradually
imposed itself—rather by the force of experience than
with the authority of a doctrine—upon the respect of
Christendom.  It had, even in modern times, been more
than once subordinated to diplomatic convenience,
overborne by ambitious rulers or misguided nations ;
but never without protest.  Far oftener, during the
nineteenth century, it had been successfully asserted
—against Napoleon, against the Turk, against the
Austrian—with the applause of Europe.  Only a few
years earlier, the cession of Savoy and Nice to France
had been submitted to a popular vote.[1]  In the case of
Alsace-Lorraine, the consent of the population was
dispensed with.  But before their nationality was taken
from them, the free institutions under which they had
lived happily allowed their protest to be heard.  The
solemn declaration of all their Deputies, elected by
a last act of citizenship, under the invader's eye, to the
Assembly at Bordeaux, records the historic refusal of
a million and a half of French citizens to become German
subjects.

Failing the consent of their new compatriots, the
victors were willing to justify the annexation upon other
grounds.  Of its military object German statesmen
made no secret.[2]  But their apologists were not content

---

[1] April 22, 1860.  There were 135,449 voters on the register:
130,839 voted ; 130,533 approved the cession.
[2] The new frontier corresponded pretty nearly with that traced
in anticipation of victory by the Prussian general staff ('the map with

to say that a strategic frontier was necessary to the new Empire, and that necessity knows no law. They appealed to history, to race, to language, to that very principle of nationalities of which the Treaty of Frankfort embodies in fact a flagrant violation.[1] With a curious pedantry they argued that Alsace-Lorraine had been an integral part of Germany until by force and fraud the French got possession of it. Its people, of German blood and German speech, had never ceased to belong to the German nation. In reclaiming them at last, united Germany was only vindicating an ancient imprescriptible right. To these allegations there is one answer which makes it unnecessary to test their accuracy. It is that since human beings are not chattels but reasonable creatures, no argument drawn from a past state of things, from kinship or from community of speech, can justify the forcible incorporation of a group of men into a system which they regard as alien, or their severance from a system which they prefer and with which they recognize their affinity. If the Alsatians and the Lorrainers had desired to become German, all other reasons would be superfluous ; since they were unwilling, no reasons whatever can avail.

The German apology has not convinced the world, but these assertions, irrelevant as they are, have undeniably impressed it. It is therefore worth while, by way of parenthesis, to qualify their crudity.

1. The question of race, for what it is worth, is not

the green border ') at an early stage of the war. The exception was the city of Belfort with the zone of its fortifications, which was finally left in French hands in exchange for the additional surrender of a few places on the Luxembourg border, particularly valuable on account of mineral wealth.

[1] *See* Mommsen's *Letters to the Italian People* (1870) and the answer of Fustel de Coulanges.

6 ALSACE-LORRAINE

settled by hasty generalization. Caesar found these
countries inhabited by Gauls and harried by Germans.
Whatever the racial significance of their incursions and
their colonies in early centuries, the Celtic strain cer-
tainly endures. In Alsace, a physical type character-
istically Gallic is met with not infrequently ; in Lorraine
it appears to predominate on either side of the present
frontier. A man from Metz looks like a man from Nancy,
and both look uncommonly like Frenchmen. It is,
besides, preposterous to forget intermarriage, as if
Alsace and Lorraine while they were parts of France had
been insulated from the rest of the country.

2. French is the mother-tongue of a few small districts
in Alsace (Schirmeck, Ste-Marie-aux-Mines, La Poutroye,
the Valley of the Bruche), and of a considerable portion
of Lorraine across the frontier, including Metz [1] and the
Pays Messin, where German, until the annexation, was
never heard. In the north-eastern corner of Lorraine,
the people speak a German dialect closely resembling
that which prevails in the Grand Duchy of Luxembourg.
Another German dialect is spoken by the immense
majority of native Alsatians. French, before the war,
was very generally spoken by the educated classes at
Strasbourg, Mulhouse, Colmar, Thionville, and in other
towns where the popular speech is Germanic. It was,
of course, everywhere understood.

3. Alsace and Lorraine, after being occupied succes-
sively by Gauls, Romans, Alamans and Franks, became
attached in the ninth and tenth centuries to the Holy
Roman Empire. Their fortunes were different. From
the fifteenth century onward the Duchy of Lorraine was

[1] I have heard the remark that Metz ' sounds German '. It is
pronounced *Messe*. *Tz* for *z* or *ts* at the end of French names is
rather common. Cf. Gretz, Batz, Beaumetz, Retz.

an autonomous and considerable state : its rulers, while acknowledging the Emperor's nominal suzerainty, alternately leaned upon the French king and quarrelled with him, and often played an active part in French affairs. Alsace, for some hundreds of years before it became French, was little more than a geographical expression, in which were included self-governing republics and the Ten Free Towns, episcopal fiefs, hereditary fiefs of the House of Austria, and counties and baronies innumerable. The morality of the several transactions by which, between 1551 and 1766, the kingdom of France acquired the two provinces, has been diversely appreciated. In the religious wars Henry II protected the Protestant princes of Germany against Charles V, and was invited by them, as a reward, to take possession of the three episcopal cities of Metz, Toul, and Verdun. After the Thirty Years' War, the Empire ceded its rights over Alsace (but in terms of singular obscurity) to Louis XIV. Strasbourg retained its virtual independence until 1681, when it was beset by the King's armies and capitulated. The Duchy of Lorraine, with that of Bar, fell peacefully to France by a kind of family arrangement. Lastly, in 1798, the little Swiss Commonwealth of Mulhouse, once included in Alsace, was at its own desire incorporated in the French Republic. It is not pretended that in any of these instances a German population was wrenched by France from a homogeneous political system. No doubt Metz in the sixteenth century, Strasbourg in the seventeenth, would have preferred a prosperous neutrality, if in those troubled times independence could have been reconciled with safety. Perhaps between Stanislas and the Revolution Lorraine sometimes regretted the desertion of its last ruler of the native line, the husband

of Maria Theresa. But it is a fact that from the first
the French kings set themselves to win the confidence
of their new subjects ; and the evidence is overwhelming
that they succeeded in a delicate task. The assimilation
of Alsace was discreet and gradual. Its governors were
in general well chosen. Its distinctive traditions and
its language were respected. Its industries were fos-
tered, and for the first time in their history its people
felt themselves secure. The Protestants of Alsace were
privileged ; so were the Jews of Metz. As for the Duchy
of Lorraine, it was in essentials French already before it
was united to the kingdom of France. What was left
to do was done by the Revolution. Lorraine and Alsace
embraced its doctrines with enthusiasm. The *Marseil-
laise* was sung for the first time in the house of the mayor
of Strasbourg. The Republican spirit indeed was in
the blood of the Strasbourgeois and of the Messin ; and
to no part of France did the extinction of feudal rights
bring greater relief than to these provinces, where so
many foreign princelings still had privileges. In the
repulse of the invader and in the Napoleonic wars Alsace
and Lorraine played a glorious part. They gave to the
French armies Ney and Kellermann, Kléber and Lefebvre,
to name no lesser heroes. And from Napoleon's fall
until the end of the French connexion, their loyalty
remained above reproach ; they were visibly prosperous,
undeniably contented ; and they contributed freely and
conspicuously to all the activities of the national life.

The Germans in 1871 had little to gain by an appeal
from the reluctance of the conquered provinces to their
remoter history ; but the past does throw some light
upon the chances with which the experiment of annexation started. Its success—a gradual moral conquest

confirming the material—would, without question, have
purchased in time the world's condonation for an abuse
of victory; and perhaps success was not impossible,
though the task was far more difficult than that which
the French monarchy assumed when it replaced a com-
plicated insecurity in old Alsace by firm and equal
government. It was not so easy for the Germans to
attach to a system which was itself upon probation
a people which had thought itself happy in its long
association with the French fortunes. And for that
heavier undertaking they had no similar aptitude. The
attractive genius of France has easily reconciled diversi-
ties of race and speech upon her borders : it is no
wonder if the Alsatians made as good Frenchmen as
Basques, or Bretons, or Flemings. But among the
German virtues that virtue of the imagination which
we call sympathy is wanting. And it seems in this
instance as if their crazy theory of race had persuaded
the conquerors that no effort on their part was needed to
accustom these new Germans to a change of nationality
which involved a change of status.

For they had been free citizens of a homogeneous
commonwealth ; and now they entered a federal system
upon an exceptional footing of subordination to its
five-and-twenty sovereign States. Alsace-Lorraine, the
ransom of France, was in this sense a pledge of German
unity, that it had been won by their joint effort under
the leadership of Prussia. By the logic of conquest it
became, not a new member of the federation, but the
common property of all. And though since 1871 the
machinery of its government has been readjusted more
than once, the most plausible ' concessions ' [1] have

[1] Until 1874 it was governed directly from the Imperial Chancellery
through an Ober-präsident at Strasbourg ; then by a Statthalter

still maintained it in the condition of a subject province, dependent (as none of the German States depend) upon the will and pleasure of the Emperor, the Federal Council, and the Imperial Parliament at Berlin. It is not certain that a real and not precarious autonomy within the Empire—such, let us suppose, as is guaranteed to the tiny principality of Reuss—would have assured the whole-hearted acquiescence of the population in the new order of things : but that was apparently the best chance, and it was not taken. Indeed it must be evident that this constitutional inequality was indispensable, if the methods of Germanization which are most agreeable to the Prussian spirit were to be employed. They may be described in two words : colonizing and repression.

An army of officials, schoolmasters, clerks, shopkeepers, artisans, from the hungrier States of the Empire, began at once to pour into the Reichsland— the grateful clients and the industrious servants of the central powers ; and the invasion did not cease when it had filled the room left vacant by the exodus of natives, of whom some thousands forsook their homes to keep their nationality. Alsace-Lorraine— economically a German dumping-ground—has been administered primarily in the interest of strangers : their growing numbers, their services, their demands,

with four Secretaries of State appointed by the Emperor. From 1874 until 1911 there was a Provincial Delegacy of 30 (later of 56) members, chosen by indirect suffrage, at first a purely consultative body, which in 1879 obtained limited powers of legislation subject to the veto of the Federal Council, but no control over the Executive. In 1911 a Constitution was granted to Alsace-Lorraine, or rather imposed upon it, by the central powers : the chief innovation was a Diet of two houses (the lower elected by the people), and the representation of the Reichsland upon the Federal Council by two Deputies —Imperial nominees.

have largely determined the policy pursued, and in particular the successive steps in the direction of legislative independence which have proved but a lure to the original population. The immigrants, however, have disappointed the hopes of the Pan-Germanists. They are still a minority; they are liable to homesickness; and they have shown themselves powerless to leaven the lump. Immigrant families, on the contrary, have been known to become good Alsatians within a generation; but, upon the whole, in all these years there has been no real contact between Wälsche (or Französling) and Schwob,[1] let alone anything like fusion.

German rule in the annexed provinces has been sometimes spoken of, with excusable exaggeration, as cruelly oppressive. It is nearer the mark to call it, in general terms, irksome, suspicious, provocative, and, above all else, incredibly tactless. For though there have been cases enough of oppression in the strict sense, it must not be supposed that the Alsatians, or even the French-speaking people of the Pays Messin, have been usually treated like mere Poles. There was even a short period when, under the first Statthalter, a Saxon—Manteuffel—a policy of conciliation, of regard for local feeling, of scrupulous impartiality, seemed about to be tried. The clamour of the Pan-Germans soon obliged the kind and courteous old soldier to repent. The charge of weakness was rebutted by acts of palpable tyranny; and it was then that the ' dictatorship clause ' was first brought into force, which allowed the executive at its sole discretion to place the Reichsland under a reign of terror. But, apart from exceptional moments, the constant spirit of the Imperial

---

[1] The Alsatian name for a German suggests that the first enemies of Alsace were Suabians.

administration has been expressed by the relentless persecution of the French language, the effacement of old landmarks, the outraging of local piety, the proscription of every emblem that could suggest the memory of happier days.  The native press has been muzzled, and a system of delation organized in every village; men have been sent to jail for whistling a tune, and women fined for wearing a ribbon or a flower; students' societies, athletic clubs, professional corporations have been broken up on suspicion of a vague Gallicizing tendency.  And the method has its comic as well as its odious side.  Zealous functionaries contributed after their kind to the Germanizing process by insisting that the Christian name of René should be registered Renatus, and by changing ' restaurant ' to ' Restauration ', and ' coiffeur ' to ' Friseur '.

Both elements were present in the notorious but not unprecedented business of Saverne, which startled all Europe at the end of 1913.  In that quiet town of Lower Alsace, an ill-conditioned Prussian subaltern provoked some effervescence by abusing the Alsatians before his men, and the military lost their heads in trying to restore order.  There was laughter—not only in Saverne—when it was known that young Hotspur could not venture so far as the pastrycook's or the tobacconist's without an escort—fixed bayonets to protect him from the jeering urchins of the place ! There was some indignation, too, about the crippled cobbler who was spitted for flouting the majesty of the Prussian uniform, and the civil notabilities who were clapped into a damp cellar for protesting.  The Strasbourg court-martial, the acquittal of the responsible chief, the Crown Prince's congratulations, were a revelation to some of us ; and our newspapers talked a good

deal at the time about North Germans and South
Germans and the overriding of civil rights by military
privilege. But the real lesson of the incident was that
in forty years and more the Prussians had made no
progress in the task of governing a province in spite
of itself, and that the subject people was not only not
assimilated, but by no means cowed.

The resistance of Alsace-Lorraine, which has never
taken the form of rebellion or of conspiracy, and has
been the more effective for that, is a consoling page
to read in recent European history. It has been maintained against all kinds of pressure by a population in
great part deprived of its natural leaders : for within
the interval allowed by the Treaty of Frankfort, most
of those who had the means to leave the country, and
many who risked their livelihood by leaving, declared
themselves Frenchmen, and sought a new home in
France, in Algeria, or abroad. Those who remained
were made more helpless by this exodus. Moreover,
the general belief that the French would soon return
was unfavourable to an active defence of their immediate
interests. For some years Alsace-Lorraine languished
in a sullen passivity, nursing its hope and its regrets,
content to express its fidelity by sending its fifteen
deputies time after time to Parliament with a single
mandate—to protest. There was some effort, in
Manteuffel's early days, to throw off this indifference
to the present ; but it was the critical period which
followed—marked as it was by frontier incidents,
trials, expulsions, domiciliary visits, the closing of
private schools, the virtual exclusion of visitors from
France—that ended by converting the provinces to
a new policy since known as Nationalism. It is the
policy of the generation which had grown up under

German rule and had got to know the Germans. Its
aim has been 'to make the house fit to live in ', while
reserving the larger question of justice for the future.
It had its centre, Colmar ; and its leaders—such men
as the Abbé Wetterlé, MM. Preiss and Blumenthal ;
and its method was a political opportunism implying
no sacrifice of sentiment, but guided by a sure sense
of reality and by the will to endure. The Nationalists
in the Reichstag and the Delegacy have consented to
form temporary alliances with German parties—the
Catholic Centre, the Social Democrats—in order to
achieve certain practical results ; the abolition of the
odious dictatorship and a relative emancipation of the
press are the most substantial of them. They could
not succeed in winning for the Reichsland a position
of complete equality with the other States ; and the
new constitution which replaced the Delegacy by
a Diet, while maintaining an irresponsible executive,
was accepted, not as a concession, but as an attempt
(which has been defeated) to crumble the particularist
opposition into groups easily absorbed by the great
divisions of German parliamentarism. But the resistance has by no means been confined to public action.
It was impossible to cut off all intercourse between
natives of the Reichsland and their kinsmen across the
frontier, or to extirpate from the soil a language which
seemed to confer a kind of aristocracy upon those who
used it. The Prussian schoolmaster with his impudent
travesties of history was no match for the Alsatian
parent ; Prussian pedantry has only stimulated the
rich and subtle humour of old Alsace.[1] In the French-

[1] It is displayed, for example, in the dialect comedy which is
a main part of the indigenous literature ; more notoriously in the
delicious caricatures of Zislin and ' Hansi ' (J.-J. Waltz—now a
French officer and serving in Alsace).

speaking districts of annexed Lorraine, where the
native population has not even the advantage of under-
standing the usurpers, nationalism has upon the whole
been less enterprising. Since Metz lost her great
bishop, Mgr. Dupont des Loges, and her valiant tribune
Antoine, the Messins, easily outnumbered by immigrants
and soldiery, have found their chief consolation in
anniversaries, in the study of their civic past and in
the pious care of graves. But such episodes as that
of ' la Lorraine sportive ' illustrate their tenacity; and
in the country-sides, where the clergy are the natural
guardians of the French tradition, even the superficial
signs of Germanization are wanting. Both provinces,
in a word, have shown themselves spiritually invincible ;
and by the experience of altered conditions in the work-
ing have grown more and more conscious of a funda-
mental incongruity between two civilizations, that
which they had irrevocably chosen, and that which
has endeavoured vainly to assimilate them.

It is sometimes asked by foreigners whether Alsace-
Lorraine would not have become a contented portion
of the German Empire if the French had frankly
accepted the result of their disasters and renounced
the hope of recovering their lost territory. The only
possible answer, for those who are familiar with the
general direction of republican policy, is that, if anything could have finally discouraged the old population
of the annexed provinces, it is the indifference to their
prospects long exhibited by official France, with the
implied assent of at least a considerable part of the
French nation. Of course it is true that for a brief
interval after the Terrible Year the eyes of nearly all
Frenchmen were fixed upon the Vosges, the Rhine, and
the Moselle. All France expected a fresh trial of strength,

and hoped for better fortune. It was the time when
every town and almost every village in France had its
little colony of exiles, among whom (to the ultimate
detriment of their cause) not a few genuine Prussians
mingled, abusing French hospitality under the shelter
of an ' Alsatian ' accent. The pathos of the case was
then liberally exploited on the stage, in fiction, in the
press, and at the tribune ; the martyrdom of the
severed brothers, their approaching rescue, the immi-
nence of *la revanche*,[1] were romantic themes, handled for
the most part somewhat childishly, and not always
perhaps with complete sincerity. It is equally true
that in the last few years French interest in Alsace-
Lorraine has once more quickened, with a better know-
ledge of the facts ; and that a revival of the old aspira-
tion has been one sure sign of recovered vitality—just
as the implicit renouncement of a whole intervening
generation had been the most depressing symptom of a
diminished national energy. Gambetta's famous 'N'en
parlons jamais, pensons-y toujours ', had announced
a policy of indefinite adjournment, and lent an air of
specious dignity to the mood of tacit resignation. The dis-
tracting influence of civil quarrels, colonial diversions,
that vague terror of Caesarism following a successful
war which long haunted the diplomacy of the Republic,
a widely diffused prosperity counselling comfortable
acquiescence, the emasculate theories of internationalists,
the fact that the centre of gravity in French politics
has shifted to a part of the country which its immunity
from invasion and its happy climate predisposed to an

---

[1] As mistranslation plays some part in international affairs, it is
worth while noting that *revanche* does not mean vengeance (' I will
repay, saith the Lord '), but ' getting even ', that is, the recovery of
a lost advantage.

amiable materialism—all these causes contributed to
keep the question of Alsace-Lorraine dormant in French
minds. It would be easy to exaggerate their apathy.
At no time have there been wanting patriots who
refused to forget or to despair. For many, as for Paul
Déroulède, the hope of reversing the decision of 1871
and of redressing the abuse of victory was a lifelong,
all-absorbing passion. His League of Patriots had no
other object. It has furnished the genius of Maurice
Barrès with its most virile inspiration. And at critical
moments (as when, in 1887, the Schnaebelé affair, which
founded Boulanger's popularity, all but precipitated
a new conflict) the attitude of the whole people showed
how thinly the old wound was cicatriced. It may be
added that no Frenchman speaking in the name of
France ever dared to use language implying a formal
acceptance of mutilated frontiers. But many, in the
interests of a political propaganda, humanitarian or
socialistic, were only too ready to profess themselves
sceptical of Alsatian sympathies.

Now and again, a hasty visit to Strasbourg has had
no other object than to corroborate surmises which
would tend to release French consciences from the
obligation of constancy. Stories of successful Germanization and a contented Reichsland were collected from
German immigrants or the rare renegades among native
Alsatians, or deduced from the negative results of an
indiscreet catechism. A bitter experience of ubiquitous
spies has made Alsatians—who are not demonstrative
by nature—less inclined than ever to wear their hearts
upon their sleeves. And the form of inquiry was often
such that an honest answer might bear an ambiguous
interpretation.—'Are you loyal to the German Empire ? '
—' We are its subjects and respect its laws ; we are

not conspirators.'—' What is your aim ? '—' To secure
justice and autonomy by constitutional means. We
want Alsace for the Alsatians.'—' Then you do not
hope to become Frenchmen again ? '—' Whatever our
preferences, we know that only the sword can make
us French. Does France desire war ? We do not.
We would rather remain as we are than that, because
of us, such a calamity should visit the two nations.'—
With such replies as these the inquisitive stranger had
to be content. Naturally, they were made the most
of by peace-mongers and Germanophils ; and provoked
a storm of protest among Alsatians in France as well
as among such other Frenchmen as had enjoyed special
opportunities of exploring the intimate predilections
of the people. But few foresaw how soon events were
to release them from their honourable reserve. All
the anguish of choice has been spared them by the
German aggression ; and no one imagines Alsace-
Lorraine disposed to cling to its masters in the hour
of their defeat.

We may now revert to the question anticipated at
the beginning of this paper, whether the case is one
for compromise. It may be said that any alternative
to pure and simple retrocession is of academic interest,
because nothing but the failure of the allied arms can
shake the resolve of the whole French people to make
the provinces, not a French possession, but a part of
France once more. Yet it is not an idle scruple which
desires to be assured that a decision in which we for
our part have no voice is one which we can applaud
without hesitation as both just and hopeful. Let us
then consider very briefly three other conceivable
solutions of the problem : complete autonomy within
the German Empire ; national independence, with

guaranteed neutrality ; the partition of the territory
and population between Germany and France.

1. The first supposes the integrity of the Empire as
at present constituted. Within it, the former Reichsland would become a Republic forming a new federal
unit. It would frame its own constitution. It would
be governed and administered by officers responsible to
the people alone. This was, before the war, the nationalist
ideal. It had no prospect of becoming a reality, and
that for reasons which the war has made more peremptory
still. For in the German (and especially the Prussian)
view, Alsace-Lorraine is a pledge of German unity, the
sign of German hegemony, and the spring-board for
a fresh attack upon France. An Alsace-Lorraine which
ceased to be that would have no value in German eyes ;
and Germany would consent to its autonomy only
with a secret resolve to reduce it as soon as possible to
the old subjection.

2. A new European State might be created—the
' buffer ' state of Alsace-Lorraine. It would be neutral,
and the Powers would guarantee its neutrality. With
the warning of Belgium before us, the prospect is not
very hopeful. A special danger would lie in the presence
of German colonists—a constant pretext for German
intervention. And there is no evidence that the people
would be satisfied with this solution. A race so eminently
military will hardly desire to be neutralized. Moreover,
the internal harmony of such a state cannot be assured.
It would not form a natural unit. The part of Lorraine
annexed in 1871 is but a fragment. Lorrainers and
Alsatians, though associated in misfortune, have little
else in common but their former status of French
citizens. In the sixteenth century, no doubt, the Duchy
of Lorraine and the little commonwealths of Alsace

would have desired no other fate than to be allowed
to live their life in complete independence of their
powerful neighbours. It is too late to-day: history
cannot be unmade.

'The first act of an Alsatian Republic', said an Alsatian
patriot recently, ' would be to declare war upon France.
France would then be forced to annex us!'

3. The Reichsland might be divided between France
and Germany. But what would be the basis of division ?
Language ? This would be mere pedantry, for speech is
no sure index of sympathies. And what would be the
fate of that portion of the country which remained
German ? If its condition were still subordinate, imagine
the reprisals that threaten the native population which
has welcomed the French army! If it received autonomy,
all the objections to the first alternative apply.

None of these, in short, is a settlement at once equitable
and likely to prove lasting. What else shall we conclude,
but that unconditional restitution will alone completely
redress the wrong done in 1871 ; alone satisfy the
inclinations of those inhabitants of Alsace-Lorraine who,
because they belong to its soil and because they have
suffered violence, have the sole right to be consulted ; [1]
and will alone put these fair countries in possession of
their full human resources by recalling to their homes
the Alsatians and Lorrainers of the dispersion ? Above
all, this is a settlement which will not be a leap in the

[1] The idea of a referendum, which has been plausibly put forward,
finds no favour among Frenchmen who reflect that, if held under
German control, it could not be considered as a test of indigenous
feeling. It would be grotesquely unfair to ask German colonists
whether they prefer that a country where they have no business
should be French or German, while the very numerous natives driven
into exile were excluded from the vote.

dark, but a return to an order of things which stood the test of many generations.

To say this is not to forget that the experiment which has failed has altered many things. Thoughtful Frenchmen are well aware that France and her lost provinces cannot meet as if they had only parted yesterday. Forty-four years of separate life have raised difficulties which did not exist before the Germans came. They believe that France can deal with them patiently and justly. There is the problem of the German immigrants. Not all of them, we may suppose, will wish to leave the country which has become their home ; there has been some—though relatively little—intermarriage between them and the old stock ; and wholesale expulsion would inflict hardship upon many innocent people. It will be the task of the Republic to mediate between the different elements of its population, and to promote their ultimate fusion. Again, the younger generation know little of France but by hearsay. The immense majority of Frenchmen have had no real contact with their former countrymen. It is inevitable that there should be surprises upon both sides. Her long insulation has undoubtedly made Alsace more than ever conscious of her distinctive moral personality, and the futile efforts of the Prussians to subdue her soul have stimulated a jealous attachment to her particular usages. French tact may be trusted to respect them. Since the French troops got a firm footing in Upper Alsace, the highest authorities have brought a message of fraternity and a promise of liberal treatment to the reclaimed districts. The responsible assurances of General Joffre and President Poincaré, like the welcome which French soldiers have found beyond the Vosges, are of the happiest augury for the future of the sturdy, refined, industrious, and reasonable people of Alsace-Lorraine, whose virtues even the rich diversity of the French temperament has sorely missed, and whose faithfulness and fortitude command the sympathy of Europe.


## SOME DOCUMENTS

1. The Declaration read, in the name of the representatives of the five departments concerned, before the French National Assembly at Bordeaux, March 1, 1871, after the vote ratifying the preliminaries of Peace :—

' Les représentants de l'Alsace et de la Lorraine ont déposé, avant toute négociation de paix, sur le bureau de l'Assemblée Nationale, une déclaration affirmant de la manière la plus formelle, au nom de ces deux provinces, leur volonté et leur droit de rester françaises.

Livrés, au mépris de toute justice et par un odieux abus de la force, à la domination de l'étranger, nous avons un dernier devoir à remplir. Nous déclarons encore une fois nul et non avenu un pacte qui dispose de nous sans notre consentement.

La revendication de nos droits reste à jamais ouverte à tous et à chacun dans la forme et dans la mesure que notre conscience nous dictera.

Au moment de quitter cette enceinte où notre dignité ne nous permet plus de siéger, et malgré l'amertume de notre douleur, la pensée suprême que nous trouvons au fond de nos cœurs est une pensée de reconnaissance pour ceux qui, pendant six mois, n'ont pas cessé de nous défendre, et d'inaltérable attachement à la patrie dont nous sommes violemment arrachés.

Nous vous suivrons de nos vœux et nous attendrons, avec une confiance entière dans l'avenir, que la France régénérée reprenne le cours de sa grande destinée.

Vos frères d'Alsace et de Lorraine, séparés en ce moment de la famille commune, conserveront à la France, absente de leurs foyers, une affection filiale, jusqu'au jour où elle viendra y reprendre sa place.'

2. GENERAL JOFFRE, at Thann, November, 1914 :—

'Notre retour est définitif, vous êtes Français pour toujours.

La France apporte, avec les libertés qu'elle a toujours représentées, le respect de vos libertés à vous, des libertés alsaciennes, de vos traditions, de vos convictions, de vos mœurs.

Je suis la France, vous êtes l'Alsace ; je vous apporte le baiser de la France.'

3. PRESIDENT POINCARÉ, at Saint-Amarin, February 12, 1915 :—

'Je viens confirmer aux populations d'Alsace les déclarations que leur a déjà faites le général Joffre. La France, heureuse d'ouvrir les bras à l'Alsace si longtemps et si cruellement séparée d'elle, ne doute pas que la victoire n'assure bientôt la délivrance des provinces qui lui ont été arrachées par la force ; et tout en respectant leurs traditions et leurs libertés elle leur rendra leur place au foyer de la patrie.'

Oxford : Horace Hart Printer to the University